Designer Barbara Zuñiga
Picture Manager Christina Borsi
Production Controller Mai-Ling Collyer
Art Director Leslie Harrington
Editorial Director Julia Charles
Publisher Cindy Richards
Indexer Hilary Bird

For photographs accompanying the recipes written
by Laura Gladwin as listed on page 128:

Photographer Adrian Lawrence
Prop stylist Luis Peral
Mixologist Michael Browne

First published in 2016 by
Ryland Peters & Small
20–21 Jockey's Fields,
London WC1R 4BW
and
341 E 116th St,
New York NY 10029
www.rylandpeters.com

10 9 8 7 6 5 4 3 2

Recipe collection compiled by Laura Gladwin
and Julia Charles.
Specially commissioned text, design and
photographs copyright © Ryland Peters & Small
2016. For full text and photography credits, see
page 128.

ISBN: 978-1-84975-779-9

Printed in China

NOTES
• Both British (Metric) and American (Imperial oz.
plus US cups) are included in these recipes for
your convenience, however it is important to work
with one set of measurements and not alternate
between the two within a recipe.
• All spoon measurements given in recipes are level
unless otherwise specified.
• Uncooked eggs should not be served to the very
old, frail, young children, pregnant women or those
with compromised immune systems. If you are
using egg whites in your cocktails, always check
the dates on the container and choose eggs with
no cracks or damaged shells.

Parisian
COCKTAILS

65 elegant drinks and bites
from the City of Light

RYLAND PETERS & SMALL
LONDON • NEW YORK

CONTENTS

A Liquid History of Paris

Paris has always been a city for drinkers. Even in Roman times, its ancient precursor Lutetia was famous for its taverns, and by the end of the seventeenth century every street in the city had at least one drinking establishment. The first cafés, including the still-famous Le Procope, appeared in the 1660s and enticed Enlightenment thinkers including Voltaire and Rousseau through their doors with radical new offerings of coffee and lemonade.

But it wasn't until the late nineteenth century that City of Light came into its own as a drinking destination. The first city to have fully electrified street lighting, still reeling from a tumultuous few decades but revelling in hitherto unseen prosperity, *la belle Paris* was both celebrated and castigated for its vice, loose morals, ruthless energy and the breathless pace of progress. It was the best place in the world to drink – and many would argue that it still is.

By 1885 there were more than 30,000 drinking dens offering a heady mix of drink, sex, ideas, arguments and revolutionary ferment. Although cocktails were already enjoying a golden age in America, in Paris the drinks of choice were wine, beer and Champagne, and few could resist the siren call of the Green Fairy herself – absinthe – which was widely available at 72% proof. This was the glorious age of the Belle Epoque, when Montmartre nightlife fizzed with activity. It was the playground of poets, artists, writers and bohemians, who met, drank, argued and philosophized, fuelled by the alcohol and music provided by cabaret bars, such as Le Chat Noir and Le Moulin Rouge, that sprang up to meet the demand. Café Les Deux Magots opened in 1885 and attracted the first of many illustrious clientèle in the form of the poets Verlaine, Rimbaud and Mallarmé, and Oscar Wilde.

The mood changed with World War I, and it was around this time that cocktails first started making their appearance in France, thanks perhaps to American troops stationed there, and the new Atlantic cruise liners connecting America with Europe, with their elegant smoking-room bars serving Manhattans and Old Fashioneds. They were still largely confined to a handful of American bars, though, notably the bar at the Hôtel Ritz Paris, which may have been one of

An early poster advertisement for Absinthe extra-supérieure.

the first hotel bars in the world. Renowned cafés La Closerie de Lilas, Le Dôme and La Rotonde were hosting the luminaries of the Parisian cultural scene on the boulevard du Montparnasse, which had by now overtaken Montmartre as the centre of literary and cultural life, particularly for young composers like Francis Poulenc, Claude Debussy, Maurice Ravel and Igor Stravinsky. French writer Guillaume Apollinaire observed that Montparnasse had become 'for artists and poets what Montmartre had been to those before them: a haven of beauty and simple freedom'.

It took the start of Prohibition in 1919 to truly launch the cocktail in Europe, though. The 1920s saw a migration of US-based artists and writers fleeing Prohibition in search of a drink in Paris, bringing with them a thirst for cocktails – and thus the exuberance of *les années folles* began. Among the greats of the so-called Lost Generation who headed for Paris were Ernest Hemingway, Scott and Zelda Fitzgerald, George Gershwin, Cole Porter, Gertrude Stein and Man Ray, and for those heady years Paris was the centre of the artistic – and cocktail – universe. For just about every sphere of cultural life, Paris was where it was at. 'If you are lucky enough to have lived in Paris as a young man then wherever you go for the rest of your life, it stays with you, for Paris is a moveable feast', Hemingway wrote in his memoir of those years. As part of his lifelong commitment to drinking, he probably set the record for the number of drinks created by or for him, including Death in the Afternoon (page 25) and the Hemingway (page 37).

The unprecedented intermingling of so many vibrant literary and cultural figures with bibulous tendencies, and the sheer sense of *joie de vivre* of a glamourous *beau monde* meeting, talking, dancing wildly and misbehaving – all fuelled by wine, Champagne, spirits and classic cocktails – has retained an intoxicating pull on the imagination ever since, most recently demonstrated in Woody Allen's 2011 film *Midnight in Paris*. As well as the favourite cafés of Montparnasse and Saint-Germain, infamous new drinking dens sprang up to cater for them, such as Harry's New York Bar, where Harry MacElhone plied his shaker to creations including the Bloody Mary (page 20), the Sidecar (page 104) and the White Lady (page 52), and jazz nightspot Le Boeuf sur le Toit, where Jean Cocteau was regularly to be found playing the drums. Several of the classic cocktails we enjoy today had their origins in this golden age of decadence.

Prohibition was repealed in 1932, but the Parisian scene remained as lively as ever and eminent figures like Coco Chanel, Yves Klein, Charlie Chaplin, among many others, continued to enjoy a Champagne cocktail or two at much-loved bars and cafés. The 1940s saw the next great flowering of the scene, this time in the area around Saint-Germain-des-Prés, home of Brasserie Lipp, Café de Flore and Les Deux Magots, and which was already hosting a thriving literary scene thanks to the number of publishers and bookshops. It now saw an explosion of small basement jazz clubs – the most infamous being Le Tabou on rue Dauphine, sadly no longer with us – playing music the world had never heard before. It was a mecca for students, struggling writers, actors, artists and musicians, many of whom met in the local cafés to work, talk and conduct their lives because their living quarters were so tiny. Most famously, this was where

The celebrated Harry's New York Bar on rue Daunou, 1920s hub of the cocktail scene.

Existentialism was born, thanks to Jean-Paul Sartre and Simone de Beauvoir, the so-called 'troglodytes of Saint-Germain'. In her memoir, Beauvoir recorded an occasion in a local bar when she and Sartre were invited by a mutual friend to philosophize about their apricot cocktails (page 63), thus kickstarting their thinking about existentialism. While Sartre seems to have preferred Scotch and soda, Beauvoir is thought to have been partial to a Gin Fizz (page 68).

Although the famous drinkers may have left, the allure of Parisian bars and cafés still burns brightly. As in many other cities, cocktails have enjoyed a resurgence in popularity in the last few decades, and there's now a vibrant scene of modish bars and speakeasies, concentrated in the Marais district, where innovative mixologists create magical concoctions – such as the Experimental Cocktail Club.

City of romance, of bright lights and chic hideaways, of afternoons whiled away in cafés on the Left Bank and strolls along the Seine, there is still no finer place than Paris for a drink – and no better inspiration to delve into your own drinks cabinet.

People & Places, Movers & Shakers

Over the centuries, Paris has boasted more watering holes – and more celebrated drinkers – than any other city in the world. The decadent years of the Belle Epoque saw a blossoming of new places to meet and drink for pleasure; as well as restaurants, bistros, brasseries, cafés and bars, there were salons, cabarets, *cafe-chantants*, *bal musettes* and *guingettes* (riverside cafés like the one made famous in Renoir's *Déjeuner de Canotiers*). These are some of the most notable bars and cafés, most of which are still open today, and the people who made them famous.

AU LAPIN AGILE, 22 RUE DES SAULES

An infamous cabaret club in Montmartre, still in (much watered-down) existence today, the Lapin Agile was frequented in its heyday by Picasso, Modigliani and Apollinaire, as well as the shadier denizens of Montmartre.

LE CHAT NOIR, 68 BOULEVARD DE CLICHY

The black cat cabaret achieved remarkable fame given that it was only open in its original form from 1881 to 1897, when its founder, Rudolphe Salis, died. Perhaps this is thanks to the iconic posters designed by Théophile Steinlen. Part literary salon, part music hall, it was one of the first cabarets in the modern sense, and a favoured haunt of *les hydropathes*, a group of radical young writers who declared themselves enemies of water, and drank only wine. It changed location several times, but always remained in Montmartre, most of whose demi-monde passed through its doors.

LE MOULIN ROUGE, 82 BOULEVARD DE CLICHY

The most famous cabaret of them all (eclipsing its rival on 32 rue Richer, the Folies Bergère), the Moulin Rouge was founded in 1889 and shocked Paris with exotic dancers doing the can-can in extravagant shows every night at 10pm. The Champagne and absinthe flowed as the owners revelled in the new-found format of an audience seated at tables and enjoying the show while being plied with food and drinks. Its enduring fame was partly down to the posters created by Toulouse-Lautrec, devoted cabaret-goer and ardent lover of absinthe – so much so that he's said to have hollowed out his walking cane and filled it with liquor.

HÔTEL RITZ PARIS, 15 PLACE VENDÔME

Founded in 1889 by César Ritz and Auguste Escoffier, the Paris Ritz was the last word in glamour and opulence. The Ritz Bar was one of the first places in Paris to serve cocktails; the Bar Hemingway is said by some to have been the birthplace of the Bloody Mary, although its ancestry is hotly contested. Legendary barman Frank Meier held court in the Ritz Bar from 1921 to 1947; he poured drinks for most of the world's glitterati during those years, from Cole Porter and Noël Coward to Coco Chanel and Franklin D. Roosevelt. The ultimate cocktail craftsman, his eccentric book *The Artistry of Mixing Drinks* is still a cult classic.

LE BOEUF SUR LE TOIT, 34 RUE DU COLISÉE

Some would say that the *années folles* began with the opening of nightclub Le Boeuf sur le Toit in 1922, which became a late-night hotspot for Jean Cocteau, Erik Satie, Coco Chanel, André Gide and countless others. On opening night, Cocteau and Darius Milhaud played the drums to an audience including Picasso, René Clair and Ballets Russes impresario Sergei Diaghilev.

LE PROCOPE, 13 RUE DE L'ANCIENNE COMÉDIE

Founded in 1686 and believed to be Paris's first café, Le Procope has welcomed an impressive list of thinkers including La Fontaine, Voltaire, Rousseau, Diderot, Benjamin Franklin, and novelists Victor Hugo and Honoré de Balzac. Even Robespierre and Danton met there during the French revolution.

A programme for the infamous Le Moulin Rouge.

BRASSERIE LIPP, 151 BOULEVARD SAINT-GERMAIN

Opened in 1880, Lipp specialized in beer and dishes from its owners' native Alsace, which Hemingway enjoyed along with a cold beer, noting that 'the *pommes à l'huile* were firm and marinated and the olive oil delicious'. It was refurbished with a beautiful Art Deco interior in 1926, including mirrors specially positioned so that every diner could see the whole restaurant. During the 1950s it was popular with artist Marc Chagall, writers Albert Camus and Françoise Sagan and singer Charles Trenet.

CAFÉ DE FLORE, 172 BOULEVARD SAINT-GERMAIN

Opened in the 1880s and a close neighbour of the more famous Les Deux Magots, fashionable Flore is now preferred over its rival by most Parisians, and was one of several beloved haunts of the American ex-pat scene.

LES DEUX MAGOTS, 6 PLACE SAINT-GERMAIN-DES-PRÈS

Perhaps *the* iconic Parisian café. Although famed as the café of intellectuals, and particularly as the headquarters of the Existentialists during the 1940s, Les Deux Magots first began life as a café in 1885, and served Oscar Wilde, James Joyce and André Breton and the Surrealists, among many others. It even launched its own literary prize, the Prix des Deux Magots, in 1933. It's still one of the best – if priciest – places to enjoy an Americano and watch the world go by.

LA COUPOLE, 102 BOULEVARD DU MONTPARNASSE

Much loved for its Art Deco interior and ornate pillars, richly decorated by artist clients, it would probably be quicker to list the members of the *beau monde* who didn't rub shoulders at La Coupole during the 1920s. Dancer Josephine Baker was a regular, along with her pet leopard Chiquita; James Joyce lined up whiskeys at the bar; in later years, Albert Camus celebrated his Nobel Prize, Patti Smith played guitar on the terrace and Serge Gainsbourg and Jane Birkin took lunch on Sundays.

LA ROTONDE, 105 BOULEVARD DU MONTPARNASSE

When La Rotonde first opened in 1911, an *anisette* cost five cents; a Pernod will now set you back €5.5. It was a particular favourite with artists and musicians – the young Debussy, Prokofiev and Stravinsky were all regulars, along with Diaghilev, Nijinsky and the Ballet Russes crowd. Modigliani, it is said, was known to sketch a portrait in return for a hot meal or a *môminette* (small glass of liquor).

American writers Ernest Hemingway and Janet Flemmer
in Les Deux Magots in 1945.

LE DÔME, 108 BOULEVARD DU MONTPARNASSE

Now famous as a seafood restaurant, Le Dôme was a valued meeting point for
the American literary colony, and is mentioned in Henry Miller's *Tropic of Cancer*
and Anaïs Nin's *Delta of Venus*. Other famous *Dômiers* included Cartier-Bresson,
Kandinsky, Lenin, Ezra Pound and Man Ray.

LA CLOSERIE DE LILAS, 171 BOULEVARD DU MONTPARNASSE

Originally set in the middle of a garden of lilacs, the Closerie attracted late-night
revellers including Emile Zola and Paul Cézanne in the closing years of the nineteenth
century. Later a particular favourite of Hemingway, who used it as an extension to his
office and wrote much of *The Sun Also Rises* there, it was also popular with Gertrude
Stein, the Fitzgeralds and Henry James. Fitzgerald and Hemingway famously
discussed *The Great Gatsby* there, no doubt over a julep or two.

HARRY'S NEW YORK BAR, 5 RUE DAUNOU

More often known simply as Harry's Bar, this was the domain of legendary
barman Harry MacElhone. Born in Scotland, he originally joined as bartender
in 1911, but bought it from its owners in 1923 and it has been in the family ever
since. Americans thirsty for a cocktail have been flocking there since the 1920s,
including the ever-present Hemingway, but also Sinclair Lewis, Jack Dempsey,
Rita Hayworth and Humphrey Bogart. George Gershwin composed *An American
in Paris* in the piano bar. Several drinks created there have since entered the
cocktail hall of fame, including the White Lady and the Sidecar.

Glossary of ingredients

ABSINTHE

A distilled spirit that has ranged in alcoholic content from around 40 to 75% ABV, depending on the manufacturer. It is flavoured with anise, fennel and wormwood (*Artemisia absinthium*), among other things, and it's the wormwood that contains the compound thujone, to which the alleged mind-bending properties are attributed. Always drunk diluted with water, absinthe is now legally available in the UK, Europe and the US.

ANGOSTURA BITTERS

A flavouring liquid for cocktails made from various aromatic herbs and botanicals distilled in alcohol. Angostura bitters have a warm and spicy flavour, and are the most famous and widely available among the many types. Once added to a cocktail, the alcoholic content of bitters is virtually nil.

ANISETTE

A liqueur flavoured with anise seeds, either by distillation or maceration. It has an ancient history in France, having been made there since the middle of the eighteenth century, but is also made in other countries including Greece and Spain. It is usually quite strong and fairly sweet; well-known brands include Marie Brizard Anisette and the Spanish Anís del Mono.

APRICOT BRANDY

One of several types of fruit brandy made by distilling a liquor from fruit juice; the same name is also given to a liqueur made from apricot flesh and kernels. One of the best-known brands is Marie Brizard Apry.

BÉNÉDICTINE

A sweet liqueur made with a top-secret combination of 27 herbs and spices. It was created in the mid-nineteenth century by a Normandy wine merchant who claimed to be reviving a centuries-old recipe for a medicinal elixir made by the local Benedictine monks.

Bottles of absinthe on sale, thanks to its recent resurgence in popularity.

CALVADOS

A type of aged apple brandy made in the Calvados region of northern France.

CHAMBORD

A brandy-based liqueur infused with raspberries and vanilla, first created in 1982 and produced in the Loire Valley in France.

CHARTREUSE

A liqueur made by Carthusian monks since 1737, based on an ancient recipe with 130 different botanical elements. It comes in the classic green and a milder yellow variety.

CRÈME DE CASSIS/FRAMBOISE/MÛRE/PÊCHE

Sweet fruit liqueurs made in France from blackcurrants (*cassis*), raspberries (*framboise*), blackberries (*mûre*) and peaches (*pêche*). The term crème refers to their rich, syrupy quality rather than creaminess.

CRÈME DE CACAO

A sweet translucent liqueur made from roasted cacao beans macerated in alcohol. Available in dark and white varieties, which have slightly different flavour profiles, but both taste essentially of dark chocolate.

CURAÇAO

A sweet liqueur originally made from the peel of a bitter and aromatic citrus fruit related to the Valencia orange, which grows on the island of Curaçao, although several types of bitter orange are now used. Triple sec, Cointreau, Grand Marnier and blue curaçao are all types of curaçao, although they are made in different ways.

DUBONNET

A French fortified wine-based apéritif infused with various herbs and spices and a small amount of quinine, first created in 1848.

GRENADINE

A non-alcoholic fruit-flavoured syrup used in cocktails. The name derives from grenade, the French word for pomegranate, and grenadine was originally made from pomegranates, although most brands these days no longer use them.

Poster advertisement for Dubonnet, c.1895.

LEMON/ORANGE ZEST TWIST

A strip of lemon or orange zest, cut thinly with a peeler so that no white pith remains attached, then twisted over the drink so that the essential oils from the zest spray on to the surface. It is generally then used to garnish the drink.

MARASCHINO

A transparent Italian liqueur made from a distillation of Marasca cherries.

MARASCHINO CHERRY

A cherry that has been preserved in sugar (not necessarily a Marasca cherry), used as a cocktail garnish. They are traditionally bright red in colour, although natural-coloured versions are available.

ORANGE BITTERS

A type of bitters (see Angostura bitters page 14) made with orange peel among other spices, with a noticeably orange flavour.

ORGEAT

A non-alcoholic syrup made from almonds and sugar, and often other flavourings such as orange flower or rose water.

PARFAIT AMOUR

A mauve-tinted, curaçao-based liqueur flavoured with a range of additions that could include some combination of violet or rose petals, almonds, lemon, coriander or vanilla.

PEYCHAUD'S BITTERS

A type of bitters (see Angostura bitters page 14) created around 1830 by an apothecary named Antoine Amédée Peychaud. They have a lighter and more floral flavour than Angostura bitters, and are traditionally used in the Sazerac.

PICON AMER

A French bitter orange apéritif liqueur, which also includes gentian and quinine, created by Gaétan Picon in the mid-nineteenth century. Also available in Picon Club and Picon Bière varieties.

SUGAR SYRUP

A basic syrup used to sweeten cocktails, also known as simple syrup. It can easily be made at home by heating two parts sugar in one part water until the sugar dissolves, then cooling and decanting into a sealed container. It keeps well in the fridge. Gomme syrup is a simple syrup with gum arabic added, which gives it a more viscous mouthfeel.

VERMOUTH

A kind of fortified wine that has been flavoured with botanical ingredients; each manufacturer's recipe is a well-guarded secret. Within the basic categories of sweet and dry, many different types exist. Traditionally, Italian vermouths are sweet and French vermouths, such as Noilly Prat, are dry, although some well-known brands, including Martini and Cinzano, make both types.

all-day cocktails

The café and restaurant were both invented in Paris, so it's no surprise that its inhabitants – and many of its celebrated visitors – have long been partial to a drink during the day. In the early days of the American cocktail, bitters were used as a tonic and mixed drinks were prescribed for restorative or soothing purposes, providing the perfect excuse for daytime imbibing. A Bloody Mary in the morning, a Mimosa before lunch, a Parisian Spring Punch with afternoon tea (perhaps not all on the same day) – what could be nicer?

Bloody Mary

Bartender Fernand 'Pete' Petiot laid claim to creating this savoury classic in at Harry's New York Bar, Paris. Well-travelled Parisian drinkers took the credit for spreading its popularity around the globe, though; Hemingway himself claimed to have introduced it to Hong Kong.

50 ML/2 OZ VODKA

150 ML/5 OZ GOOD-QUALITY TOMATO JUICE

10 ML/2 TEASPOONS FRESHLY SQUEEZED LEMON JUICE

7 ML (ABOUT 3 DASHES) WORCESTERSHIRE SAUCE

3 DASHES TABASCO

1 LARGE PINCH SALT

1 LARGE PINCH FRESHLY GROUND BLACK PEPPER

A CELERY STICK AND A SLICE OF LEMON, TO GARNISH

Fill a cocktail shaker with ice cubes, then add the vodka, tomato juice, lemon juice, Worcestershire sauce, Tabasco, salt and pepper. Shake well and strain into a chilled highball glass. Garnish with a celery stick and a slice of lemon. Serve immediately.

Mimosa

A bartender at the Hôtel Ritz Paris is thought to have invented the Mimosa around 1925. Whoever came up with it, it was a devilishly good idea to pair Champagne with virtuous orange juice and suggest that we drink it with brunch.

10 ML/2 TEASPOONS GRAND MARNIER
75 ML/3 OZ (ABOUT ½ GLASS) CHAMPAGNE
FRESHLY SQUEEZED ORANGE JUICE, TO TOP UP

Pour the Grand Marnier into a chilled Champagne flute, add the Champagne and orange juice and stir gently. Serve immediately.

A quintessentially Parisian view – Le Tour Eiffel.

Parisian Spring Punch

This delightfully appley sparkler would be just the thing to revive the spirits over brunch, perhaps with a macaron or two, after an early-morning stroll in the Tuileries.

25 ML/1 OZ CALVADOS

15 ML/½ OZ DRY VERMOUTH

DASH OF FRESHLY SQUEEZED LEMON JUICE

DASH OF SUGAR SYRUP

WELL-CHILLED CHAMPAGNE, TO TOP UP

LEMON ZEST AND FRESH MINT SPRIGS, TO GARNISH

Fill a collins or highball glass with ice cubes. Pour in the Calvados, vermouth, lemon juice and sugar syrup and stir well. Top with Champagne. Garnish with a twist of lemon zest and a sprig of mint, add straws and serve.

Scott and Zelda Fitzgerald
were regulars at La Coupole for
breakfast – washed down with
Champagne, of course.

Sherry Cobbler

The Sherry Cobbler was one of the earliest cocktails to catch on in nineteenth-century America, and was equally happy across the pond in Paris. It was often made in a punch bowl to be doled out at social gatherings. Vary the fruits as you please — berries would be inauthentic, but nice.

50 ML/2 OZ DRY SHERRY, SUCH AS FINO OR AMONTILLADO

10 ML/2 TEASPOONS FRESHLY SQUEEZED LEMON JUICE

10 ML/2 TEASPOONS FRESHLY SQUEEZED ORANGE JUICE

10 ML/2 TEASPOONS SUGAR SYRUP

15 ML/½ OZ PINEAPPLE JUICE OR PURÉE

THIN LEMON AND ORANGE SLICES, TO GARNISH

Fill a cocktail shaker with ice cubes, add all the ingredients except the citrus slices and shake well. Strain into a chilled tumbler or highball glass filled with crushed ice. Garnish with slices of lemon and orange and serve with a straw.

Death in the Afternoon

One of Hemingway's cocktail creations, the recipe for this one advised readers to 'drink three to five of these slowly'. The editor of the 1935 book it appeared in observed: 'it takes a man with hair on his chest to drink five … and still handle the English language in the Hemingway fashion'.

35 ML/1½ OZ ABSINTHE

ABOUT 125 ML/5 OZ VERY COLD CHAMPAGNE

Pour the absinthe into a chilled Champagne flute and top gently with the Champagne. It will turn milky and opalescent. Serve immediately.

As well as the famous wormwood, which contains the compound responsible for the hallucinogenic symptoms, absinthe is flavoured with liquorice, hyssop, fennel and angelica.

Brandy Flip

Dating from an era when cocktails were still prescribed for their medicinal qualities, this one was served for soothing effect in the morning or afternoon — most likely after an energetic evening at the white-hot 1920s cabaret bar, Le Boeuf Sur la Toit.

50 ML/2 OZ COGNAC

10 ML/⅓ OZ SINGLE/LIGHT CREAM

5 ML/1 TEASPOON SUGAR SYRUP

1 EGG, LIGHTLY BEATEN

**FRESHLY GRATED NUTMEG,
TO GARNISH (OPTIONAL)**

Half-fill a cocktail shaker with ice cubes and add all the ingredients except the nutmeg. Shake well and strain into an old-fashioned glass or brandy balloon. Dust the top with a little grated nutmeg and serve.

(Note that it's a good idea to check that the intended imbiber is happy to drink raw egg, see note on page 4.).

A Parisian barman shakes a cocktail for his audience c.1929.

apéritifs & champagne cocktails

There's nothing better than a chilled cocktail to enliven the appetite and set the scene before a meal. The cocktail hour is a subject in which France has long specialized, with apéritif inventions like the Kir and Kir Royale, as well as spirits and fortified wines like Picon, Pernod, Lillet and Pineau des Charentes. Champagne cocktails, from the Saint Germain to the Hemingway, are light, irresistibly celebratory and the perfect start to any evening.

Classic Champagne Cocktail

The classic Champagne cocktail has been giving pleasure to drinkers in Paris and around the world for decades, and it's still just perfect for channelling a little Moulin Rouge-style decadence.

25 ML/1 OZ BRANDY
1 WHITE SUGAR CUBE
SEVERAL DASHES OF ANGOSTURA BITTERS
WELL-CHILLED DRY CHAMPAGNE, TO TOP UP

Chill the brandy first by swirling it gently in a glass with ice cubes. Place the sugar cube in a chilled Champagne flute and moisten it with the Angostura bitters. Add the brandy, then gently pour in the Champagne and serve immediately.

the Metropolis

Perhaps inspired by the Parisian café classic Kir Royale, the Metropolis combines Champagne with the same appealing berry flavours, but adds a kick of vodka to give it a steely edge.

25 ML/1 OZ VODKA

25 ML/1 OZ CRÈME DE FRAMBOISE

WELL-CHILLED DRY CHAMPAGNE, TO TOP UP

Fill a cocktail shaker with ice cubes and add the vodka and crème de framboise. Shake well and strain into a chilled cocktail glass. Top with Champagne and serve immediately.

French 75

Unlikely as it sounds, this was named for the 75mm gun used by the French in World War I. It was popular at Harry's New York Bar, so feel free, while you sip, to imagine yourself in the company of Hemingway and the Fitzgeralds; perhaps that's Picasso with Gertrude Stein over there...

25 ML / 1 OZ GIN
10 ML / 2 TEASPOONS FRESHLY SQUEEZED LEMON JUICE
5 ML / 1 TEASPOON SUGAR SYRUP
WELL-CHILLED DRY CHAMPAGNE, TO TOP UP
LEMON ZEST, TO GARNISH

Fill a cocktail shaker with ice cubes, add the gin, lemon juice and sugar syrup and shake well. Strain into a chilled Champagne flute. Top with Champagne and garnish with a long strip of lemon zest. Serve immediately.

Saint Germain

A delicious and sprightly summer sparkler, perfect for imaginatively transporting yourself to the cafés of Saint-Germain-des-Prés where Jean-Paul Sartre and Simone de Beauvoir held court.

50 ML/2 OZ WELL-CHILLED DRY CHAMPAGNE

35 ML/1½ OZ ELDERFLOWER LIQUEUR, SUCH AS ST-GERMAIN

SODA WATER, TO TOP

LEMON ZEST, TO GARNISH

Fill a collins glass or tall tumbler with ice cubes. Add the Champagne and elderflower liqueur and top with soda water. Stir gently and garnish with a long strip of lemon zest. Serve immediately.

At the opulent grand opening
of La Coupole café in
December 1927, a staggering
1,200 bottles of Champagne
were quaffed.

Kir

This classic café apéritif actually originated in Dijon and is traditionally made with the local blackcurrant liqueur, crème de cassis, and Bourgogne Aligoté wine, but any light, dry white wine will do nicely.

25 ML/1 OZ CRÈME DE CASSIS

175 ML/6 OZ WELL-CHILLED DRY WHITE WINE

Pour the crème de cassis into a wine glass, add the white wine and serve immediately. Crème de pêche (peach) or crème de mûre (blackberry) liqueurs make very nice variations.

Kir Royale

The more luxurious cousin of the Kir, the upscale Royale — like its relative — is utterly straighforward to make, and is delicious at any time of day. *Tout simple.*

20 ML / ¾ OZ CRÈME DE CASSIS

ABOUT 125 ML / 4½ OZ WELL-CHILLED DRY CHAMPAGNE

Add a small dash of crème de cassis to a chilled Champagne flute and gently top with Champagne. Stir gently and serve immediately.

The ornate design of Perrier-Jouët's famous Belle Epoque Champagne bottle was created by Emile Gallé, a French glass artist and one of the leading lights of the Art Nouveau style, in 1902.

Pernod
(classic serve)

Perhaps *the* classic French apéritif, anise-flavoured Pernod was developed when the much stronger absinthe was temporarily banned in 1915, allowing Parisians to carry on enjoying that inimitable flavour of the Belle Époque.

ABOUT 50 ML/2 OZ PERNOD

ABOUT 250 ML/9 OZ WELL-CHILLED WATER

Pour the Pernod into a tumbler and serve with a carafe of well-chilled water and a bowl of ice cubes. Leave your fellow drinkers to add water and ice to taste, letting each person create that always-satisfying transition from clear to cloudy. The standard ratio of one part Pernod to five parts water is a good place to start.

Hemingway

A delight for lovers of both Hemingway and Pernod, this combines two of Papa's favourite tipples. It's a lighter way to try Hemingway's classic (but fiercer) cocktail creation Death in the Afternoon (see page 25), especially if you have plans to do anything afterwards.

25 ML/1 OZ PERNOD

ABOUT 125 ML/5 OZ WELL-CHILLED DRY CHAMPAGNE

1 STAR ANISE, TO GARNISH (OPTIONAL)

Pour the Pernod into a chilled Champagne flute. Top up with Champagne. Garnish with the star anise, if using, and serve immediately.

the Americano

Named for the American troops stationed in Italy during the World War I, the Americano quickly became a popular apéritif in Parisian boulevard cafés — still probably the best place to drink one.

25 ML/1 OZ CAMPARI
25 ML/1 OZ SWEET VERMOUTH
SODA WATER, TO TOP UP
ORANGE OR LEMON SLICE, TO GARNISH

Fill a highball glass with ice cubes, pour in the Campari, vermouth and soda water, then stir. Add an orange or lemon slice and stir, then serve immediately.

During the 1920s golden age of cocktails, vodka was little known in America, and wasn't much used until the return of the American expatriates from Paris when Prohibition was repealed in 1933.

Le Moulin Rouge with its iconic red windmill in a postcard c1910.

Amer Picon Cocktail

Amer Picon, a French bitter orange liqueur made with gentian and quinine that dates back to the early nineteenth century, was a popular ingredient during the 1920s and 30s, the golden age of cocktails. This is a great way to rediscover its charms.

50 ML/2 OZ AMER PICON

10 ML/⅓ OZ GRENADINE

35 ML/1½ OZ FRESHLY SQUEEZED LIME JUICE

Fill a cocktail shaker with ice cubes and add all the ingredients. Shake well, strain into a chilled cocktail glass and serve immediately.

Bière Picon

A less well-known but equally classic French apéritif, this transforms any beer into a rather chic thirst-quencher, ideal for watching the world go by at Les Deux Magots. Look out for the type of Picon labelled Picon Bière; if you can't find it, Amer Picon will do.

25 ML/1 OZ PICON BIÈRE OR AMER PICON
WELL-CHILLED LAGER, TO TOP

Pour the Picon into a stemmed beer glass and top with cold lager. Serve immediately.

Tourboats cruise down the River Seine at sunset.

the *Impressionist*

What nicer way to relive the heady atmosphere of the Boulevard des Capucines in 1874, where the soon-to-be-called Impressionists held their first joint exhibition? The luscious scents of raspberry and violet evoke the joyous colours of Monet's garden.

15 ML / ½ OZ GRAND MARNIER CHERRY
15 ML / ½ OZ RASPBERRY SYRUP (IDEALLY HOME MADE)
5 ML / 1 TEASPOON MICLO VIOLETTE LIQUEUR
WELL-CHILLED DRY CHAMPAGNE, TO TOP UP

Fill a cocktail shaker with ice cubes. Add the Grand Marnier cherry, raspberry syrup and violette liqueur and shake well. Strain into a chilled cocktail glass and top up with Champagne. Serve immediately.

The first official ascent of the newly built Eiffel Tower took place on 31 March 1889, when 300 of the workmen feasted and drank Champagne on the first platform.

gin and vodka cocktails

Aromatic and versatile with a flinty core, gin was the original spirit of choice for most cocktails. Many of the classics are based on it, from Slings to Gimlets to Fizzes to Rickeys, all delicious and refreshing in their simplicity. Vodka was a more recent development, but is now an essential addition to the liquor shelf for most bartenders. Clean-tasting and effortlessly chic (F. Scott Fitzgerald claimed to prefer gin because he said it left no trace on his breath), gin and vodka cocktails accommodate themselves to nearly any situation.

Music Hall Théâtre

Moulin Rouge

Programme   OUVERT TOUTE L'ANNÉE
50 cent.   DIRECTION :
Jean FABERT

French Leave

A delicious Gallic twist on the classic Screwdriver, this is said to have become popular among American GIs taking leisurely leave in France. A devilish variation with absinthe in place of the Pernod would also be worth considering!

25 ML/1 OZ VODKA
25 ML/1 OZ PERNOD
100 ML/3½ OZ FRESHLY SQUEEZED ORANGE JUICE
AN ORANGE SLICE, TO GARNISH

Fill a cocktail shaker with ice cubes and add the vodka, Pernod and orange juice. Shake well and strain into a chilled cocktail glass. Garnish with a slice of orange and serve immediately.

A modern-day barman prepares drinks at the iconic Harry's Bar, Paris.

Pépa

This racy number is named after Pépa Bonafé, a French film starlet who appeared alongside the legendary Josephine Baker in the 1927 movie *La Revue des Revues*, about a chorus girl who becomes the darling of the Parisian nightclub scene.

35 ML/1½ OZ DRY VERMOUTH

25 ML/1 OZ COGNAC

25 ML/1 OZ VODKA

DASH OF ANGOSTURA BITTERS

LEMON ZEST, TO GARNISH

Fill a cocktail shaker with ice cubes and add the vermouth, cognac, vodka and bitters. Stir well and strain into a chilled cocktail glass. Garnish with a twist of lemon zest and serve immediately.

A Beaux Arts-style bridge connects the Champs-Elysées with the Eiffel Tower

White Lady

The White Lady, the epitome of pale elegance, is the creation of bartender Harry MacElhone, who originally made it with crème de menthe; he replaced this with gin at Harry's New York Bar, Paris, in the 1920s. The egg white lends her a deliciously silky glamour, but it's not essential.

25 ML/1 OZ FRESHLY SQUEEZED LEMON JUICE

25 ML/1 OZ COINTREAU

35 ML/1½ OZ GIN

½ EGG WHITE (OPTIONAL)

Fill a cocktail shaker with ice cubes and add all the ingredients. Shake very well, then strain into a chilled cocktail glass. Serve immediately.

Ernest Hemingway, a man who took drinking very, very seriously, once wrote: 'I drink to make other people more interesting.'

Marguerite

This less well-known but extremely *soignée* cousin of the Martini would be just the thing to order should you ever find yourself whisked back in time, *Midnight in Paris*-style, to a 1920s Parisian bar.

35 ML/1½ OZ GIN

25 ML/1 OZ DRY VERMOUTH

15 ML/½ OZ ORANGE CURAÇAO

DASH OF ANGOSTURA BITTERS

ORANGE ZEST, TO GARNISH

Fill a cocktail shaker or large tumbler with ice cubes and add the gin, vermouth, orange curaçao and Angostura bitters. Stir well and strain into a chilled cocktail glass. Garnish with a twist of orange zest and serve immediately.

The name of the famous Les Deux Magots café comes from the two stocky Chinese figurines, or *magots*, who look out over the room.

Cocktail Bleu

The celebrated Parisian café La Coupole created a Cocktail Bleu in 1958 to celebrate 'Exposition du Vide', an exhibition by Yves Klein, artist and creator of the iconic colour International Klein Blue. This version is a twist on the classic White Lady created at Harry's New York Bar, Paris.

35 ML / 1½ OZ GIN
15 ML / ½ OZ BLUE CURAÇAO
15 ML / ½ OZ COINTREAU
1 TEASPOON FRESHLY SQUEEZED LEMON JUICE
1 TEASPOON SUGAR SYRUP
ORANGE ZEST, TO SERVE (OPTIONAL)

Fill a cocktail shaker with ice cubes, add all the ingredients and shake well. Strain into a chilled cocktail glass, add a twist of orange zest, if using, and serve immediately.

Sapphire

Who can resist a perfect love? Parfait Amour is a curaçao-based, mauve-tinted liqueur infused with rose petals or violets and almonds, and it adds a seductive *je ne sais quoi* to the austerity of very cold gin.

10 ML / 2 TEASPOONS PARFAIT AMOUR

50 ML / 2 OZ WELL-CHILLED GIN

FRESH BLUEBERRIES, TO GARNISH

Make sure you chill the gin in the freezer before starting. Gently pour the Parfait Amour into a well-chilled cocktail glass. Pour in the gin over the rounded back of spoon, so that it forms a layer over the Parfait Amour. Garnish with blueberries on a cocktail stick and serve immediately.

Parisian Martini

Bartending legend Harry MacElhone, founder of Harry's New York Bar, Paris, included this simple but delicious blackcurrant-infused apéritif in his influential 1927 book *Barflies and Cocktails*. He named it simply 'Parisian Cocktail', and it showcases two of France's best-known liquors.

35 ML / 1½ OZ GIN

35 ML / 1½ OZ DRY VERMOUTH

35 ML / 1½ OZ CRÈME DE CASSIS

LEMON ZEST, TO GARNISH

Fill a cocktail shaker with ice cubes and add the gin, vermouth and crème de cassis. Stir well and strain into a chilled cocktail glass. Garnish with a twist of lemon zest and serve.

French Martini

Made with Chambord, a French raspberry liqueur apparently inspired by one drunk by King Louis XIV, this simple, fruity 1980s invention helped start the craze for calling anything in a martini glass a Martini.

50 ML/2 OZ VODKA
15 ML/½ OZ CHAMBORD
50 ML/2 OZ FRESH PINEAPPLE JUICE

Fill a cocktail shaker with ice cubes and add all the ingredients. Shake very well and strain into a chilled cocktail glass. Serve immediately.

Gin Gimlet

'A popular beverage in the Navy', declared Harry MacElhone in *Barflies and Cocktails*, no doubt because the sweet, scurvy-scotching lime made the gin ration more palatable. A simple and strengthening apéritif.

50 ML/2 OZ GIN

25 ML/1 OZ LIME CORDIAL, SUCH AS ROSE'S

Fill a cocktail shaker with ice cubes and add the gin and lime cordial. Shake very well and strain into a chilled cocktail glass, or an old-fashioned glass filled with ice. Serve immediately.

Cucumber Basil Gimlet

A fresh, modern variation on the classic — perfect for sipping during a game of pétanque on the Paris Plage.

75 ML/3 OZ GIN

15 ML/½ OZ LIME CORDIAL, SUCH AS ROSE'S

5 BASIL LEAVES, TORN

5 CUCUMBER SLICES, CHOPPED

CUCUMBER SPEAR, TO GARNISH

Fill a cocktail shaker with ice cubes and add all the ingredients except the cucumber spear. Shake very well and strain into a chilled cocktail glass. Garnish with a cucumber spear. Serve immediately. (See photo left.)

Gin Rickey

The Gin Rickey will forever be associated with F. Scott Fitzgerald, thanks to the 'four gin rickeys that clicked full of ice' in *The Great Gatsby*. A regular in the bars and cafés of 1920s Paris, Fitzgerald wrote in another novel, *The Beautiful and the Damned*, 'Here's to alcohol, the rose-colored glasses of life'.

60 ML/2½ OZ GIN

15 ML/½ OZ FRESHLY SQUEEZED LIME JUICE

8 ML/1½ TEASPOONS SUGAR SYRUP (OR TO TASTE; PURISTS WOULD DRINK IT WITHOUT)

SODA WATER, TO TOP UP

LIME ZEST, TO GARNISH

Fill a cocktail shaker with ice cubes and add the gin, lime juice and sugar syrup, if using. Shake and strain into an ice-filled highball glass. Top up with soda. Garnish with a long strip of lime zest. Serve immediately.

Zaza

Named after an 1898 French play that was made into a film several times — a rags-to-riches tale of a music-hall entertainer who becomes the mistress of an aristocrat — the darkly glamorous Zaza more than does justice to two of its stars, Gloria Swanson and Claudette Colbert.

35 ML/1½ OZ GIN

35 ML/1½ OZ DUBONNET

DASH OF ANGOSTURA BITTERS

A MARASCHINO CHERRY OR ORANGE ZEST, TO GARNISH

Fill a cocktail shaker with ice cubes and add the gin, Dubonnet and bitters. Stir well and strain into a chilled cocktail glass. Garnish with a maraschino cherry or twist of orange zest and serve immediately.

Apricot Cocktail

It's possible that a cocktail inspired French existentialism: Simone de Beauvoir and Jean-Paul Sartre were drinking apricot cocktails at a Parisian bar in 1932 when a friend opened their eyes to phenomenology by asking if they could analyse their drinks. It's not known exactly what they drank, but it's fun to speculate!

35 ML/1½ OZ APRICOT BRANDY

2 TEASPOONS FRESHLY SQUEEZED LIME JUICE

2 TEASPOONS FRESHLY SQUEEZED LEMON JUICE

5 ML/1 TEASPOON GIN

DASH OF SUGAR SYRUP

Fill a cocktail shaker with ice cubes and add all the ingredients. Shake well and strain into a chilled cocktail glass. Serve immediately.

Gin Sling

One of the earliest styles of cocktail, a sling is basically a spirit mixed with sugar and water. It has given rise to endless variations, and every Paris bartender worth his salt would have had his own version.

FRESHLY SQUEEZED JUICE OF ½ A LEMON

12.5 ML/2½ TEASPOONS SUGAR SYRUP

35 ML/1½ OZ GIN

15 ML/½ OZ CHERRY BRANDY

SODA WATER, TO TOP UP

Fill a cocktail shaker with ice cubes and add all the ingredients except the soda water. Shake vigorously and strain into a chilled highball glass. Top up with soda water and serve immediately.

Raspberry Tom Collins

This is a lovely, fruity twist on the Tom Collins, another cocktail classic brought to Paris by the American ex-pats of the 1920s, no doubt much to the delight of the locals. It was originally made with Old Tom, a slightly sweeter and smoother style of gin.

50 ML/2 OZ GIN, PREFERABLY OLD TOM

25 ML/1 OZ FRESHLY SQUEEZED LEMON JUICE

12.5 ML/½ OZ RASPBERRY PURÉE

12.5 ML/½ OZ SUGAR SYRUP

SODA WATER, TO TOP UP

FRESH RASPBERRIES, TO GARNISH

Fill a cocktail shaker with ice cubes and add all the ingredients except the soda water and raspberries. Shake well and stain into a highball glass filled with ice. Top up with soda water and stir, then garnish with raspberries. Serve immediately.

The optimal amount of time to shake a cocktail for is 12 seconds; by this time, the ideal temperature of between -5 and -8 °C (or 23 and 18°F) will have been reached.

Lucien Gaudin

This orange-spiked twist on a Negroni was created in honour of the dashing French Olympic fencing champion of the same name. Gaudin, who died in Paris after a duel in 1934, was said to be one of the greatest classical fencers of the twentieth century.

35 ML/1½ OZ GIN

15 ML/½ OZ CAMPARI

15 ML/½ OZ COINTREAU

15 ML/½ OZ DRY VERMOUTH

ORANGE ZEST, TO GARNISH

Fill a cocktail shaker or large tumbler with ice cubes and add all the gin, Campari, Cointreau and vermouth. Stir well and strain into a chilled cocktail glass. Garnish with a twist of orange zest and serve immediately.

An inviting neon sign adorns a bar on the rue de Seine, Left Bank.

Ramos Gin Fizz

The classic Gin Fizz, which is very similar to the Tom Collins, is still on the menu of Le Dôme café on boulevard Montparnasse. This popular version, created in New Orleans in 1888, includes egg white and cream for a richer texture.

50 ML/2 OZ GIN

25 ML/1 OZ DOUBLE/HEAVY CREAM

½ AN EGG WHITE

15 ML/½ OZ FRESHLY SQUEEZED LIME JUICE

10 ML/⅓ OZ FRESHLY SQUEEZED LEMON JUICE

12.5 ML/½ OZ SUGAR SYRUP

3 ML (2 DASHES) ORANGE-FLOWER WATER

A SLICE OF LEMON, TO GARNISH

Fill a cocktail shaker with ice cubes and add all the ingredients. Shake vigorously for as long as you can, then shake some more. Strain the mixture into a chilled highball glass and garnish with a slice of lemon. Serve immediately.

The ice in cocktail shakers has two important functions: to chill the liquid down, and to dilute the spirits slightly, which helps open up the flavours.

Gin Fizz Royale

A decadent take on the Gin Fizz, fit for Parisian royalty. Gin Fizzes were especially popular in the 1940s — so much so that some bars had to hire extra bartenders to handle all the shaking.

25 ML/1 OZ FRESHLY SQUEEZED LEMON JUICE

1 EGG WHITE

50 ML/2 OZ GIN

15 ML/½ OZ SUGAR SYRUP

CHILLED CHAMPAGNE, TO TOP UP

A SLICE OF LEMON, TO GARNISH

Fill a cocktail shaker with ice cubes and add the lemon juice, egg white, gin and sugar syrup. Shake vigorously, then strain into a highball glass filled with ice. Top with Champagne and garnish with a slice of lemon. Serve immediately.

the Martinez

The Martinez is a precursor of the Martini, which wasn't drunk widely during Prohibition, possibly because of the poor quality of bootlegged gin and the wider availability of sweet Italian vermouth. The Martinez may have held more appeal for the tastebuds of the time.

50 ML/2 OZ GIN
15 ML/½ OZ ITALIAN VERMOUTH
1 DASH ORANGE BITTERS
1 DASH MARASCHINO
A LEMON ZEST TWIST, TO GARNISH

Fill a cocktail shaker with ice cubes and add all the ingredients except the garnish. Stir well and strain into a chilled cocktail glass. Garnish with a twist of lemon zest and serve immediately.

Ce Soir ou Jamais

This strong and racily titled concoction (in English, Tonight or Never) was included in the book *Cocktails de Paris*, published in 1929 at the height of the Parisian cocktail fad. The original recipe calls for Marie Brizard Apry as the apricot brandy, and it's well worth seeking out.

25 ML/1 OZ GIN
25 ML/1 OZ DRY VERMOUTH
10 ML/⅓ OZ COGNAC
10 ML/⅓ OZ APRICOT BRANDY

Fill a cocktail shaker with ice cubes and add all the ingredients. Stir well and strain into a chilled cocktail glass. Serve immediately.

Mixed drinks first started to become popular in France in the early 1860s, when the phylloxera epidemic killed off most of the vineyards, dramatically reducing wine production.

rum and whiskey cocktails

Rum and whiskey cocktails, with their enticing aura of long, hot evenings, crisply tailored suits, classic cocktail bars and spirited conversation, are some of the most seductive drinks of all. The straightforward but impeccable Manhattans and Old-Fashioneds, as well as the more flamboyant Juleps and Daiquiris, were beloved by some of the most renowned Parisian drinkers.

Mint Julep

Think of a Mint Julep and you can't help thinking of long, hot, steamy summers in the 1930s, possibly with F. Scott Fitzgerald characters arguing in the background. There's no better drink to kick off a balmy evening, full of promise.

ABOUT 12 FRESH MINT LEAVES, PLUS MINT SPRIGS TO GARNISH
7 ML/1½ TEASPOONS SUGAR SYRUP
50 ML/2 OZ BOURBON

Put the mint leaves and sugar syrup in a highball glass or julep cup and muddle them together well. Fill the glass with crushed ice and add the bourbon. Stir well with a long spoon until the outside of the glass frosts. Garnish with mint sprigs and serve immediately.

Peach Julep

Most people don't realise that the very first Juleps, which were among the first American cocktails to become popular internationally, were made with cognac and peach brandy instead of the bourbon. Try it in this delicious variation.

ABOUT 10 FRESH MINT LEAVES, PLUS A MINT SPRIG TO GARNISH

¼ RIPE PEACH, CUT INTO WEDGES, PLUS A SLICE TO GARNISH

15 ML/½ OZ PEACH BRANDY, SUCH AS MARIE BRIZARD PEACH LIQUEUR

50 ML/2 OZ COGNAC (OR USE BOURBON)

Put the mint, peach wedges and peach brandy in a cocktail shaker and muddle together well. Add the cognac and shake well. Strain into a highball glass or julep cup filled with crushed ice and stir well. Garnish with a mint sprig and slice of peach and serve immediately.

F. Scott Fitzgerald, whose enthusiasm for alcohol was as high as his tolerance was low, observed that: 'First you take a drink, then the drink takes a drink, then the drink takes you.'

Original Daiquiri

This simple classic was invented in the 1890s by an American mining engineer in Cuba, and was made famous by the bartenders of Havana. Different styles of rum will need different amounts of lime and sugar, so adjust the recipe until you find the perfect combination.

50 ML/2 OZ LIGHT RUM
20 ML/¾ OZ FRESHLY SQUEEZED LIME JUICE
1–2 TEASPOONS SUGAR SYRUP, TO TASTE
LIME WEDGE, TO GARNISH (OPTIONAL)

Fill a cocktail shaker with ice cubes and add all the ingredients except the garnish. Shake well and strain into a chilled cocktail glass. Garnish with the lime wedge, if using, and serve immediately.

Hemingway Daiquiri

Created at El Floridita, Havana, for the legendary cocktail muse Ernest Hemingway, aka Papa Doble (so called because he always ordered a double). He liked it without sugar, but most people prefer the addition of the syrup.

35 ML / 1½ OZ WHITE RUM
10 ML / 2 TEASPOONS MARASCHINO
15 ML / ½ OZ GRAPEFRUIT JUICE
15 ML / ½ OZ FRESHLY SQUEEZED LIME JUICE
15 ML / ½ OZ SUGAR SYRUP

Fill a cocktail shaker with ice cubes, add all the ingredients and shake well. Strain into a chilled cocktail glass and serve immediately.

Although whiskey and soda is the most frequent drink in Hemingway's books, Saint-James rum was what he mentioned drinking most often in *A Moveable Feast*, his memoir of his time in Paris.

Boulevardier

This moody version of the Negroni, based on rye whiskey, was named after the 1920s Parisian literary magazine *The Boulevardier*. It was edited — and the drink was downed — by Erskine Gwynne, American ex-pat and socialite, member of the illustrious Vanderbilt family and Harry's Bar regular.

35 ML/1½ OZ RYE WHISKEY
25 ML/1 OZ CAMPARI
25 ML/1 OZ SWEET RED VERMOUTH
ORANGE SLICE, TO GARNISH

Fill an old-fashioned glass with ice cubes. Pour in the whiskey, Campari and vermouth and stir well. Add an orange slice and serve immediately.

The word 'cocktail' made its first appearance in print in America 1806, when it was defined as 'a stimulating liquor, composed of spirits of any kind, sugar, water and bitters.'

Between the Sheets

This potent number is thought to have first been mixed by Harry MacElhone at Harry's New York Bar, Paris, in the early 1920s. It's proof that drinkers enjoyed a saucy cocktail name then just as much as we do now; the trend even extended to the now-best-forgotten Bosom Caresser.

25 ML/1 OZ BRANDY
25 ML/1 OZ LIGHT RUM
25 ML/1 OZ ORANGE LIQUEUR, SUCH AS COINTREAU OR TRIPLE SEC
10 ML/2 TEASPOONS FRESHLY SQUEEZED LEMON JUICE

Fill a cocktail shaker with ice cubes and add all the ingredients. Shake well and strain into a chilled cocktail glass. Serve immediately.

Angostura bitters were invented as a stomach tonic, and are named after the town of Angostura in Venezuela, although they're now made in Trinidad and Tobago.

Old-Fashioned

How many cocktails can claim to be the subject of a Cole Porter song? 'Make it Another Old-Fashioned, Please' was written for the heroine of Paris-ophile Porter's 1940 musical *Panama Hattie*. Opinions differ on whether the fruit should be muddled, and some bartenders prefer to omit the cherries.

1 WHITE SUGAR CUBE

1–2 ORANGE SLICES

1–2 MARASCHINO CHERRIES (OPTIONAL)

2 DASHES ANGOSTURA BITTERS

SPLASH OF WATER

50 ML/2 OZ BOURBON

Put the sugar, one orange slice, one cherry and the Angostura bitters in an old-fashioned glass. Muddle them together very well until the sugar has dissolved, then remove the orange rind. Add the bourbon, water and ice cubes and stir very well. Garnish with the remaining orange slice and cherry (if using) and serve immediately.

Manhattan

One of the earliest cocktails, the Manhattan's lineage dates back to the 1880s. The original version used sweet vermouth; later, in the 1920s and 30s, the Dry Manhattan — made with French vermouth — was more popular. The Perfect Manhattan uses equal quantities of sweet and dry vermouth.

50 ML/2 OZ BOURBON
25 ML/1 OZ SWEET RED VERMOUTH
2 DASHES ANGOSTURA BITTERS
A MARASCHINO CHERRY OR TWIST OF ORANGE ZEST, TO GARNISH

Fill a cocktail shaker with ice cubes, add all the ingredients except the garnish and stir well. Strain into a chilled cocktail glass, garnish with a cherry or a twist of orange zest and serve immediately.

One of the earliest known cocktail books to be published in France was *Bariana: Recueil pratique de toutes boissons americains et anglaises* in 1896, and it contains a few classics we still recognize today: the Martini, the Manhattan and the Champagne Cocktail.

Parisian Blonde

Another classic from the 1920s, this would be perfect for sipping at the bar of the Hôtel Ritz Paris, your (fake) mink stole slipping elegantly from your shoulders. Many versions include a shot of cream, which makes for a rich but delectable digestif.

20 ML / ¾ OZ DARK RUM, PREFERABLY JAMAICAN

20 ML / ¾ OZ LIGHT RUM

20 ML / ¾ OZ COINTREAU

20 ML / ¾ OZ SINGLE/LIGHT CREAM (OPTIONAL)

ORANGE ZEST, TO GARNISH (OPTIONAL)

Fill a cocktail shaker with ice cubes and add all the ingredients. Shake well and strain into a chilled cocktail glass. Garnish with a twist of orange zest, if using, and serve immediately.

Hôtel Paris Ritz bartender Frank Meier advised: 'A cocktail should always be perfect. There is no reason ever to drink a bad one.'

Whisky Sour

James Joyce, who spent 20 years in Paris and whose great modernist novel *Ulysses* was first published there in 1922, may well have enjoyed one of these to celebrate at the bar of La Coupole. No doubt his were made with Irish 'whiskey', though.

50 ML/2 OZ SCOTCH WHISKY

25 ML/1 OZ FRESHLY SQUEEZED LEMON JUICE

12.5 ML/½ OZ SUGAR SYRUP

½ EGG WHITE (OPTIONAL)

**A FRESH CHERRY AND
A SLICE OF LEMON, TO GARNISH**

Fill a cocktail shaker with ice cubes and add all the ingredients except the garnish. Shake vigorously, ideally for at least 30 seconds (longer if you leave out the egg white). Strain into a chilled old-fashioned glass and garnish with a cherry and a slice of lemon. Serve immediately.

Vieux Carré

Named after the French Quarter of New Orleans, this is a scintillating marriage of French and American ingredients — rather like Paris in the 1920s. Use extra Angostura if you can't find Peychaud's bitters.

3 DASHES ANGOSTURA BITTERS
3 DASHES PEYCHAUD'S BITTERS
10 ML/2 TEASPOONS BÉNÉDICTINE
25 ML/1 OZ BOURBON
25 ML/1 OZ SWEET RED VERMOUTH
25 ML/1 OZ COGNAC
ORANGE ZEST, TO GARNISH

Pour all the ingredients over ice in a mixing jug/pitcher. Stir with a bar spoon. Remove the ice and put in an old-fashioned glass. Pour the cocktail into the glass; add more ice if needed to top up. Garnish with the orange twist and serve immediately.

A couple enjoying the Jardin de Tuileries on a misty day, c.1945.

digestifs and late-night drinks

Along with apéritifs, digestifs are the other area in which France has excelled: from fortifying Cognac and Armagnac to aromatic herbal liqueurs like Chartreuse, there are plenty of ways to send down a good meal. The classic B&B (Bénédictine and brandy) is a great way to start. Wormwood-infused absinthe has to be the ultimate late-night drink, though – sip a Green Fairy or Absinthe Suissesse after midnight and you'll be in estimable company.

Absinthe

The classic way to serve absinthe — as it would have been served in the *fin de siècle* bars of Montmartre — takes a little patience and paraphernalia, but it's worth it for the magical moment of the *louche*, when the absinthe emulsfies with the water and turns opalescent.

50 ML/2 OZ ABSINTHE

1 CUBE WHITE SUGAR

WELL-CHILLED WATER, IN A CARAFE

You'll need an absinthe spoon, or a straining spoon with holes in it, or (at a pinch) a metal coffee or tea strainer. Pour the absinthe into a small stemmed glass. Place the sugar cube on the spoon and position it over the glass. Drip the water slowly onto the cube so that the sugar dissolves through the strainer into the glass. Stir gently, adding a little more water if necessary to reach a ratio of approximately 3 parts water to 1 part absinthe (according to taste). Serve immediately.

Oscar Wilde observed of drinking absinthe: 'The first stage is like ordinary drinking, the second when you begin to see monstrous and cruel things, but if you can persevere you will enter in upon the third stage where you see things that you want to see, wonderful curious things.'

Absinthe Frappé

This refreshing way to drink absinthe, a version of which was developed by that great bartender of 1920s Paris, Harry MacElhone, was probably inspired by the traditional method of serving it (see left). It makes for a lighter and longer drink.

25 ML/1 OZ ABSINTHE

15 ML/½ OZ ANISETTE

5 ML/1 TEASPOON SUGAR SYRUP

SODA WATER, TO TOP UP

Fill a cocktail shaker with ice and add the absinthe, anisette and sugar syrup. Shake well and strain into a chilled old-fashioned glass or small tumbler filled with crushed ice. Top up with soda water, add straws and serve immediately.

Degas' famous painting *L'Absinthe*, which shows a female friend drinking in a Parisian café, scandalized English society when it was first exhibited in 1893 – many critics felt it was not an appropriate subject for a painting.

Absinthe Suissesse

In his 1927 classic *Barflies and Cocktails*, Harry MacElhone declared that the Absinthe Suissesse 'is a very good bracer for that feeling of the morning after the night before', and who are we to argue with the maestro?

50 ML/2 OZ ABSINTHE

15 ML/½ OZ ORGEAT

15 ML/½ OZ EGG WHITE

15 ML/½ OZ SINGLE/LIGHT CREAM (OPTIONAL)

MINT LEAVES, TO GARNISH

Fill an old-fashioned glass with crushed ice. Fill a cocktail shaker with ice cubes and add all the ingredients except the mint leaves. Shake well, then strain into the glass. Garnish with mint leaves and serve immediately.

Green Fairy

The 'green fairy' (*la fee verte*), the venerable nickname for absinthe, was much more than just a drink: to the bohemians and poets of 1890s Paris she was an artists' muse, a symbol of transformation and inspiration. All of which is a perfect excuse to drink one of these…

25 ML/1 OZ ABSINTHE

25 ML/1 OZ FRESHLY SQUEEZED LEMON JUICE

25 ML/1 OZ CHILLED WATER

20 ML/¾ OZ SUGAR SYRUP

DASH OF ANGOSTURA BITTERS

½ EGG WHITE

Fill a cocktail shaker with ice cubes and add all the ingredients. Shake very well and strain into a chilled cocktail glass. Serve immediately.

B&B

Created in 1937, this simple digestif combines two of France's most sophisticated liquors to produce a late-night tipple worthy of any existentialist debate à la Sartre and de Beauvoir. It's also good served straight up at room temperature in a brandy balloon.

35 ML/1½ OZ BRANDY

35 ML/1½ OZ BÉNÉDICTINE

LEMON ZEST, TO GARNISH (OPTIONAL)

Fill a brandy balloon or an old-fashioned glass with ice cubes. Add the brandy and Bénédictine, stir and add the lemon zest twist, if using. Serve immediately.

Deauville

This delicious apple twist on the classic Sidecar was named after the fashionable seaside resort of Deauville, capital of the Calvados region of Normandy and centre of the Parisian Riviera. High-society Parisians have been flocking there on their summer holidays for decades.

25 ML/1 OZ CALVADOS
25 ML/1 OZ COGNAC
25 ML/1 OZ TRIPLE SEC
10 ML/2 TEASPOONS FRESHLY SQUEEZED LEMON JUICE
A DASH OF SUGAR SYRUP

Fill a cocktail shaker with ice cubes, add all the ingredients and shake well. Strain into a chilled cocktail glass and serve immediately.

A New Yorker columnist reported Jean-Paul Sartre as having said: 'Two phrases only are necessary for a whole evening of English conversation, I have found: "Scotch-and-soda?" and "Why not?" By alternating them, it is impossible to make a mistake'.

Brandy Alexander

Smooth, luxurious and rather soignée, the Brandy Alexander was invented in the 1920s; like so many cocktails, its exact origins are disputed, but it appears in Harry MacElhone's 1927 *Barflies and Cocktails*. It's the perfect digestif for Parisian sophisticates.

50 ML/2 OZ BRANDY
25 ML/1 OZ DARK CRÈME DE CACAO
25 ML/1 OZ DOUBLE/HEAVY CREAM
GRATED NUTMEG, TO GARNISH

Fill a cocktail shaker with ice cubes and add all the ingredients except the nutmeg. Strain into a chilled cocktail glass, dust with the nutmeg and serve immediately.

Silk Stocking

This irresistibly named, pale blush-coloured cocktail is definitely best drunk after midnight in an elegant Parisian club. It also works well shaken with ice and strained into a cocktail glass.

35 ML/1½ OZ GOLD TEQUILA

15 ML/½ OZ WHITE CRÈME DE CACAO

15 ML/½ OZ DOUBLE/HEAVY CREAM

5 ML/1 TEASPOON GRENADINE

2 FRESH RASPBERRIES, TO GARNISH

Put all the ingredients except the raspberries in a blender, add 2 handfuls of ice cubes and blend for 20 seconds. Pour the mixture into a chilled hurricane glass, garnish with the raspberries and serve immediately with straws.

Writer, designer and artist Jean Cocteau embodied the spirit of jazz age Paris, and some credited him with popularizing American cocktails, noting the similarity between his name and 'cocktail'.

Espresso Martini

The perfect wake-up call after a decadent dinner. It's fun to speculate that Sergei Diaghilev, the colourful Russian impresario who made such a splash in 1909 Paris with the Ballets Russes, might have enjoyed one of these.

50 ML/2 OZ FRESHLY BREWED ESPRESSO, COOLED
50 ML/2 OZ VODKA
1 DASH SUGAR SYRUP, OR TO TASTE
3 COFFEE BEANS, TO GARNISH

Fill a cocktail shaker with ice cubes and add the coffee, vodka and sugar syrup. Shake vigorously and strain into a chilled cocktail glass. Garnish with the coffee beans and serve immediately.

Almond Espresso Martini

This delectable twist on the espresso martini is ideal for anyone who prefers their drinks a little sweeter. Hemingway would certainly have disapproved.

25 ML/1 OZ FRESHLY BREWED ESPRESSO, SWEETENED TO TASTE AND COOLED

35 ML/1½ OZ VODKA

20 ML/¾ OZ AMARETTO

15 ML/½ OZ KAHLÚA

3 COFFEE BEANS AND A PINCH OF TOASTED, SLIVERED ALMONDS, TO GARNISH

Fill a cocktail shaker with ice cubes and add all the ingredients except the garnish. Shake well and strain into a chilled cocktail glass. Wait for the cocktail to separate: a foam will rise to the top and the liquid below will become clearer. Garnish with the coffee beans and toasted almonds and serve immediately.

Pousse-Café

The *pousse-café*, or 'coffee pusher', was created to help send the post-prandial coffee on its way (and, no doubt, to showcase the virtuosity of the bartender). When poured carefully, the liqueurs will form layers according to their relative densities.

GRENADINE

DARK CRÈME DE CACAO

MARASCHINO LIQUEUR

CURAÇAO

GREEN CRÈME DE MENTHE

PARFAIT AMOUR

COGNAC

In a chilled tall shot glass, champagne flute or pousse-café glass, pour a small measure of each of the ingredients, one on top of the other, in the order they are listed. Pour each one very slowly over the rounded back of a teaspoon or barspoon that is touching the side of the glass. Leave to stand for a few moments to help the layers equalize, then serve immediately.

Champs-Elysées

A suitably grand cocktail, and fortifying enough for a stroll up the infamous Parisian boulevard. The sweet herbal liqueur Chartreuse has been made by French Carthusian monks since the early eighteenth century, and comes in green and yellow varieties; either can be used here.

50 ML / 2 OZ COGNAC
15 ML / ½ OZ CHARTREUSE
15 ML / ½ OZ FRESHLY SQUEEZED LEMON JUICE
5 ML / 1 TEASPOON SUGAR SYRUP
A DASH OF ANGOSTURA BITTERS
LEMON ZEST, TO GARNISH

Fill a cocktail shaker with ice cubes and add the cognac, Chartreuse, lemon juice, sugar syrup and bitters. Shake well and strain into a chilled cocktail glass. Garnish with a lemon zest twist and serve immediately.

Chic Parisians enjoying a drink at a busy pavement café.

Fontainebleau Special

Another cocktail that celebrates a favourite Parisian getaway, this lovely digestif is named for the region of Fontainebleau just outside the capital, which is famous for its large oak forest. Perhaps the herbal notes of the anisette carry a fragrant hint of its woodland delights.

35 ML / 1½ OZ COGNAC
35 ML / 1½ OZ ANISETTE
15 ML / ½ OZ DRY VERMOUTH

Fill a cocktail shaker with ice cubes and add all the ingredients. Shake well and strain into a chilled cocktail glass. Serve immediately.

For many artists and writers of the *Belle Epoque*, alcohol was a potent metaphor for inspiration. As Charles Baudelaire wrote in his poem Be Drunk, 'It is time to be drunk! … On wine, on poetry or on virtue as you wish.'

Sazerac

One of the earliest cocktails, the Sazerac was invented in the 1850s, and it's still an excellent after-dinner drink. Back then it was made with cognac, and replacing the rye whiskey with cognac gives it an interesting twist.

ABSINTHE OR PASTIS, TO RINSE THE GLASS

50 ML/2 OZ RYE WHISKEY OR COGNAC

10 ML/2 TEASPOONS SUGAR SYRUP

2 DASHES BITTERS, PREFERABLY PEYCHAUD'S

LEMON ZEST, TO GARNISH

Chill an old-fashioned glass and fill another one with ice cubes. Rinse the chilled glass with the absinthe or Pernod. Add the remaining ingredients, except the lemon zest, to the ice-filled glass and stir very well. Strain into the absinthe-rinsed glass, garnish with a thin strip of lemon zest and serve immediately.

Sidecar

Another classic with disputed origins, although most agree it was invented around the end of World War I. The great Paris bartender Harry MacElhone was certainly one of the first to write it down; his version contained equal parts brandy, lemon and Cointreau, but most modern versions increase the amount of brandy.

SUGAR, TO RIM THE GLASS, OR ORANGE ZEST, TO GARNISH (OPTIONAL)

50 ML/2 OZ BRANDY

20 ML/¾ OZ FRESHLY SQUEEZED LEMON JUICE

20 ML/¾ OZ COINTREAU

If using the sugar garnish, moisten the rim of a chilled cocktail glass and dip it into sugar to create a rim. Fill a cocktail shaker with ice cubes and add the ingredients. Shake well, strain into the chilled cocktail glass, garnish with the orange zest (if using) and serve immediately.

Pear Sidecar

A chic pear variation of the Sidecar that makes good use of the lovely
eau de vie Poire Williams.

SUGAR, TO RIM THE GLASS
30 ML/1½ OZ BRANDY
30 ML/1½ OZ PEAR BRANDY, PREFERABLY POIRE WILLIAMS
25 ML/1 OZ FRESHLY SQUEEZED LEMON JUICE
A THIN SLICE OF PEAR, TO GARNISH

If using the sugar garnish, moisten the rim of a chilled cocktail glass and dip it into sugar to create a rim.
Fill a cocktail shaker with ice cubes and add the ingredients. Shake well and strain into the cocktail glass.
Garnish with the slice of pear and serve imediately.

Enjoying the early evening sunshine at a Montmartre café, c1949.

amuse bouche

A nibble is always welcome with a well-made cocktail. These recipes offer a little taste of Paris in the form of salty anchovies and tangy olive tapenade, creamy *chèvre* and buttery flaky pastry. From light snacks including spiced nuts and popcorn, to more substantial bar bites, such as a rich pâté with apricots and vermouth-infused scallops, the perfect *amuse bouche* for the cocktail hour is here.

Spiced Mixed Nuts

These nuts are incredibly moreish and perfect served with any of the cocktails in this book. You may want to keep them hidden in a cupboard to stop yourself constantly nibbling!

500 G/5 CUPS ASSORTED UNSALTED NUTS (CASHEWS, HAZELNUTS, BRAZIL NUTS, PEANUTS, BLANCHED ALMONDS, PECANS, WALNUTS)

1 TABLESPOON FENNEL SEEDS

15 G/2 TABLESPOONS SESAME SEEDS

100 G/¾ CUP PUMPKIN SEEDS

1½ TABLESPOONS (ABOUT 2 SPRIGS) COARSLEY CHOPPED FRESH ROSEMARY

1 TEASPOON DRY RED CHILLI/HOT PEPPER FLAKES

4 TEASPOONS DARK MUSCOVADO SUGAR

1 TEASPOON SEA SALT

2 TABLESPOONS MELTED UNSALTED BUTTER

MAKES ABOUT 450 G/4 CUPS

Preheat the oven to 180°C (350°F) Gas 4.

Mix the nuts together in a bowl and then spread on a baking sheet. Toast in the preheated oven for about 10 minutes, until lightly golden brown. Keep a close eye on them though as the nuts can burn quickly.

Meanwhile, place the fennel, sesame and pumpkin seeds in a preheated frying pan/skillet set over a medium heat. Dry fry the seeds for a few minutes until the sesame seeds turn lightly golden brown.

Put the rosemary, chilli/hot pepper flakes, sugar, salt and melted butter in a large mixing bowl and stir to combine. While the nuts and seeds are still warm from the oven and pan, toss in the butter spice mixture to coat thoroughly. Serve warm or at room temperature.

Spicy Popcorn

100 G / 3½ OZ CORN KERNELS
2 TABLESPOONS SUNFLOWER OIL
3 TABLESPOONS MELTED UNSALTED BUTTER
½ TEASPOON SEA SALT
½ TEASPOON SMOKED PAPRIKA
¼ TEASPOON CAYENNE PEPPER

1 large lidded saucepan at least 24 cm/9 ½ inches diameter and 13 cm/5 inches deep

MAKES 1 LARGE BOWL

Put the corn and the oil into a pan and spread the kernels out to make an even layer. Cover with a lid and cook on the hob/stovetop over medium-high heat.

When the kernels start popping, shake the pan a few times to distribute the heat. The kernels will only take a few minutes to cook, any longer and they will catch and start to burn.

Tip the popcorn into a large bowl and drizzle over the melted butter. Sprinkle with the salt, paprika and cayenne pepper, toss well and serve.

Blue Cheese and Walnut Cocktail Biscuits

These tasty, crumbly little treats make great pre-dinner nibbles served with a cocktail for sipping. Freshly chopped chives make a lovely addition to the recipe, too.

90 G/6 TABLESPOONS BUTTER, SOFTENED

130 G/4½ OZ STRONG BLUE CHEESE, SUCH AS ROQUEFORT

200 G/1⅓ CUPS PLAIN/ALL-PURPOSE FLOUR

A PINCH OF SEA SALT

50 G/⅓ CUP WALNUTS, CHOPPED

2 baking sheets, lined with baking parchment

MAKES ABOUT 30

Preheat the oven to 180°C (350°F) Gas 4.

Beat the butter and blue cheese together in a large mixing bowl until evenly mixed. Work in the flour and salt and bring the mixture together to form a smooth dough. Add the chopped walnuts and knead very lightly until they have all been evenly combined.

Form the mixture into two long sausage shapes and wrap both tightly in clingfilm/ plastic wrap. Refrigerate for 30 minutes or so to firm up.

Unwrap the dough and cut into slices just under 1 cm/³/₈ inch thick. Arrange on the prepared baking sheets, leaving a little space for spreading between each one.

Bake in the preheated oven for 10–12 minutes, until crisp and golden. Leave to cool for 5 minutes or so, before transferring to a wire rack to cool completely before serving.

Fennel Seed Crackers with Chèvre and Honey

If you love the aniseed flavour of fennel seeds these delicate little crackers are perfect for you and make the ideal accompaniment to any absinthe-based drinks.

120 G/1 CUP PLAIN/ALL-PURPOSE FLOUR

½ TEASPOON BAKING POWDER

½ TEASPOON SALT

4 TABLESPOONS WATER

3 TABLESPOONS OLIVE OIL

2 TEASPOONS FENNEL OR ANISE SEEDS, CRUSHED USING A PESTLE AND MORTAR, PLUS 1 TEASPOON TO DECORATE

2 TABLESPOONS CASTER/GRANULATED SUGAR

150 G/5½ OZ GOATS' CHEESE/CHÈVRE

RUNNY (IDEALLY FRENCH) HONEY, FOR DRIZZLING

A FEW SPRIGS OF FRESH THYME

a baking sheet, lined with baking parchment

a chefs' blowtorch

MAKES 40

Preheat the oven to 180°C (350°F) Gas 4. Mix all the ingredients together to make a dough. Tip the dough out onto a floured surface and roll it until it is 2 mm/^{1}/$_{16}$ inch thick. Cut the dough into 5-cm/2-inch disks.

Put the disks onto the prepared baking sheet and cook in the preheated oven for 12 minutes. Remove from the oven, sprinkle with caster/granulated sugar. Use the chefs' blowtorch to caramelize the surface.

Leave the crackers to cool on a wire rack. Once the crackers are cool, spread with a little goats' cheese/chèvre, drizzle with honey and place a thyme sprig on each one. Serve as soon as you can.

Variation: For a speedier and no less delicious bite, spread wholewheat or rye crackers with a herbed soft cheese (such as Boursin) and top with a sun-dried tomato and a sprig of fresh dill.

Vermouth Scallops with Olive Tapenade

Considered an indulgent treat, scallops served on a slice of *saucisson* make a surprisingly simple-to-prepare and satisfying hot bite to enjoy at cocktail hour.

20 FRESH SCALLOPS

1½ TABLESPOONS DRY FRENCH VERMOUTH

1 TABLESPOON OLIVE OIL

45 G/⅔ CUP GREEN OLIVES, PITTED/STONED

1–2 LARGE SPRING ONIONS/ SCALLIONS, CHOPPED

1 SMALL GARLIC CLOVE

1 TABLESPOON FRESHLY CHOPPED FLAT-LEAF PARSLEY

150 G/5 OZ CURED FRENCH SAUSAGE (SAUCISSON)

SALT AND FRESHLY GROUND BLACK PEPPER

a griddle pan

cocktail sticks

MAKES 20

Put the scallops in a large bowl with 1 tablespoon of the vermouth, the olive oil and a pinch of salt and black pepper and let sit for 10 minutes.

Heat a griddle pan over high heat until very hot and sear the scallops for a minute on each side. Do not move the scallops during cooking, or they will tear.

Put all the remaining ingredients, except the sausage, in a food processor with $1/2$ teaspoon salt and give it a few short sharp blasts until the tapenade mixture looks chopped but not too mushy. Slice the sausage so you have a slice for each scallop (not too thinly as you want it to support the weight of the scallops).

To assemble, spoon a little tapenade onto each sausage slice, put a seared scallop on top and secure with a cocktail stick and serve hot.

Crab Toasts with Radish Salsa

Fresh crab is delicious in its own right, so serve this fresh and tangy chive, caper and radish salsa in a bowl with a small serving spoon so that you can add some to each mouthful.

1 SLIM BAGUETTE/FRENCH STICK

500 G/1 LB FRESH CRABMEAT

200 G/7 OZ FROMAGE FRAIS/SOUR CREAM

radish salsa:
200 G/7 OZ FRENCH BREAKFAST RADISHES, SCRUBBED AND ROUGHLY CHOPPED

70 G/½ CUP CAPERS, DRAINED AND CHOPPED

A HANDFUL OF FRESH CHIVES, VERY FINELY CHOPPED

4 TABLESPOONS OLIVE OIL

4 TABLESPOONS SWEET GINGER WINE

2 baking sheets

MAKES 40

Preheat the oven to 200°C (400°F) Gas 6.

Slice the baguette/French stick into 40 even slices. Arrange on baking sheets in the oven for about 10 minutes, turning once, until nicely browned.

Gently combine the fresh crabmeat and fromage frais in a bowl and chill. When you are ready to serve, mix all the salsa ingredients together in a separate bowl. Use a small palette knife to spread the cold crab mixture onto the toasts, then top with a little salsa. Serve as soon as you can or the toasts will become soggy.

Pork Rillettes

Rillettes are like a French pâté with a bit more texture, because the meat is shredded, rather than puréed. Serve at room temperature, with some Melba toast, this is a special canapé, and very easy to make. Just the thing to accompany a glass of Kir.

200 G/7 OZ PORK BELLY (RINDLESS), TRIMMED AND DICED

1 TABLESPOON SEA SALT

2 TABLESPOONS BUTTER

1 GARLIC CLOVE, FINELY CHOPPED

A SMALL PINCH OF GROUND MACE

1 BAY LEAF

1 TABLESPOON FRESHLY CHOPPED FLAT-LEAF PARSLEY, PLUS EXTRA TO SERVE

50 ML/SCANT ¼ CUP DRY WHITE WINE

150 ML/⅔ CUP CHICKEN STOCK

SALT AND FRESHLY GROUND BLACK PEPPER

FRESHLY SQUEEZED LEMON JUICE, TO SERVE

MELBA TOAST AND CORNICHONS/PICKLE SPEARS, TO SERVE

2 ramekins, or other small pots

SERVES 2

Put the pork belly in a non-metallic container and sprinkle the sea salt over the top. Massage the salt into the meat, then cover tightly and refrigerate for 1–2 hours. Rinse and dry the pork cubes — the salt should have already drawn some of the moisture out of the pork belly, but you don't want to draw out too much because you're going to slow-cook it, which will benefit from keeping the fat.

Melt the butter in a saucepan over medium heat, then add the pork belly, garlic, mace, bay leaf and parsley, and season with salt and pepper. Cook, stirring often, to slightly brown the pork and coat it in the seasoning, then add the white wine and keep increase the heat to high for 1–2 minutes to reduce the wine. Pour in the chicken stock.

Turn the heat down to very low and cover. Leave it cooking gently for $1^1/_4$ hours. At this stage, press one of the cubes of pork with a fork and if it starts to fall apart, it's had long enough. If the mixture is starting to dry out and stick to the bottom of the pan, just add another splash of chicken stock — about 50 ml/scant $^1/_4$ cup. Replace the lid and leave to cook gently for another 20—30 minutes if necessary, until the meat is falling apart.

Remove from the heat and leave to cool. Discard the bay leaf. Let the pork cool enough to handle, then pull it apart with your (clean) fingers and mix it really well. If you have a large piece of fat on its own, remove it, but the fat should have mostly melted. Transfer the pork to the ramekins and chill in the refrigerator for at least 1 hour so that the mixture can set. Bring it out of the refrigerator about 30 minutes before serving to allow the flavour to develop. Serve with melba toasts and cornichons/pickles spears.

Pâté with Dried Apricots and Pistachios

In this recipe the sweetness from the apricots is a lovely contrast to the richness of the chicken livers, and the texture, with the pistachio nuts, is really pleasing.

3½ TABLESPOONS BUTTER

½ RED ONION, CHOPPED

½ GARLIC CLOVE, CHOPPED

75 G/3 OZ PORK BELLY (RIND REMOVED), DICED

200 G/7 OZ CHICKEN LIVERS, CHOPPED

1 TABLESPOON FRENCH BRANDY OR COINTREAU

60 G/2½ OZ READY-TO-EAT DRIED APRICOTS, CHOPPED

15 G/½ OZ SHELLED PISTACHIO NUTS

1 TEASPOON FRESHLY SQUEEZED LEMON JUICE

SALT AND FRESHLY GROUND BLACK PEPPER

FINELY SLICED READY-TO-EAT DRIED APRICOTS AND PISTACHIOS, TO DECORATE

OATCAKES, TO SERVE

4 ramekins, or other small pots

SERVES 4

Heat a generous 1 tablespoon of the butter in a frying pan/skillet set over medium heat, until melted. Add the red onion and garlic, and fry on their own for 1 minute. Add the pork belly, chicken livers and brandy, season with salt and pepper, and stir. Cook, stirring regularly for 10 minutes, until everything is browned and the pork belly and chicken livers are cooked through.

Remove from the heat and let cool until the mixture is warm, not hot — don't let it cool completely, otherwise the ingredients will dry out.

Put the mixture into a food processor (don't wash the pan yet), add the apricots, pistachio nuts and the squeeze of lemon juice, and whizz.

You can keep this mixture chunky so that you still get a bite of apricot and the soft crunch of pistachio in the pâté, or you can blitz until smooth, if you prefer. Spoon the mixture into the ramekins and level the surface of each one so that the melted butter can go on top.

In the same frying pan/skillet you were using before, melt the remaining butter over medium heat, until it starts to bubble, and then remove from the heat and pour over the top of the pâté. Decorate with slices of dried apricot and slivers of pistachio. Put the pâté in the refrigerator and the butter will set in about 1 hour. Serve with oatcakes.

The pâté will keep in the refrigerator for 1 week, if the butter is unbroken on the top. Eat within 3 days once you have broken through the butter seal.

Gougères

These cheese-enriched choux pastry puffs are a classic French bar bite — perfect enjoyed with any of the cocktails in this book or simply a glass of wine.

50 G/3 TABLESPOONS BUTTER, CUBED

75 G/½ CUP PLAIN/ ALL-PURPOSE FLOUR, SIFTED WITH ¼ TEASPOON SALT AND A PINCH OF CAYENNE PEPPER

3 EGGS

50 G/½ CUP FINELY GRATED WELL-MATURED GRUYÈRE

2 baking sheets, lightly greased

MAKES 20–24

Preheat the oven to 220°C (425°F) Gas 7. Measure 150 ml/^{2}/$_3$ cup water into a large saucepan and add the butter. Heat gently until the butter has melted, then bring to the boil. Remove from the heat. Add the sifted flour mixture.

Beat vigorously with a wooden spoon until the mixture forms a ball and leaves the side of the pan clean. Set aside for 5 minutes. Beat 2 eggs and gradually add them to the pastry, working them in until the mixture is smooth and glossy. Add all except 1 heaped tablespoon of the cheese. Run the baking sheets under the tap and then shake off any excess water.

Place teaspoonfuls of the mixture onto each baking sheet. Beat the remaining egg and brush the top of each puff lightly with a pastry brush. Sprinkle with the remaining cheese. Bake in the preheated oven for about 25 minutes until puffed up and golden. Remove the gougères from the oven and cut a small slit in the base of each to let the hot air escape. Let cool on a wire rack before serving.

Anchovy Wafers

Ready-made salty snacks pall beside these crumbly melt-on-the-tongue wafers. They deserve to be paired with a glass of well-chilled dry Champagne.

125 G/1 CUP PLAIN/ALL-PURPOSE FLOUR

125 G/1 STICK CHILLED BUTTER, CUBED

125 G/1¼ CUPS MATURE/SHARP CHEDDAR, GRATED

2 TEASPOONS DRIED OREGANO

100 G/4 OZ ANCHOVIES IN OLIVE OIL, DRAINED AND HALVED LENGTHWAYS

FRESHLY GROUND BLACK PEPPER

2 baking sheets

MAKES ABOUT 40

Sift the flour onto a clean work surface, make a well in the centre and add the butter, cheese, oregano and black pepper.

With clean, cool fingers, rub together to form a soft, tacky dough. Scoop the dough up, with the aid of a spatula if necessary, and put it on a large piece of baking parchment. Mould the mixture into a flattish rectangle, wrap up in the paper and chill for 1 hour in the fridge.

Preheat the oven to 200°C (400°F) Gas 6.

Using a sharp knife, cut the dough (just as you would slice a loaf of bread) into thin wafers and arrange them on baking sheets, positioning them not too close together. Lay an anchovy half lengthways on each wafer and bake for 8 minutes until golden. Let cool on a wire rack before serving.

Crèmes Brûlées

Rich, creamy vanilla custard topped with crisp caramel is the epitome of Parisian chic —
enjoy for dessert with a brandy-based cocktail to sip alongside.

600 ML/2⅔ CUPS DOUBLE/HEAVY CREAM

1 VANILLA BEAN, SPLIT

6 EGG YOLKS

100 G/½ CUP SUGAR, PLUS 2 TABLESPOONS TO DUST

1 TEASPOON ICING/CONFECTIONERS' SUGAR

4 large ramekins

chefs' blowtorch (optional)

MAKES 4

Preheat the oven to 150°C (300°F) Gas 2.

Put the cream and vanilla bean in a saucepan over low heat and bring to the boil. Meanwhile, put the egg yolks and sugar in a mixing bowl and whisk with a balloon whisk until light and fluffy. Slowly pour the boiled cream into the egg mixture, whisking vigorously until evenly incorporated.

Pass the mixture through a fine sieve/strainer and discard the vanilla bean and any bits of unwelcome egg shell. Divide the custard mixture between the ramekins and place them in a deep roasting pan. Pour water into the pan to reach halfway up the sides of the ramekins. This is called a 'bain marie' and will ensure that the crème brûlées bake evenly and gently.

Bake in the preheated oven for 40—45 minutes. There should still be a slight wobble in the middle of the crèmes brûlées when you shake them gently.

Remove the crèmes brûlées from the oven, take them out of the roasting pan and allow to cool completely. You can then refrigerate them until needed, if you like. When you are ready to serve them, dust the 2 tablespoons sugar over them, followed by the icing/confectioners' sugar. The sugar will give you crunch and the icing/confectioners' sugar will give you shine.

You can now caramelize the tops of the crèmes brûlées using a chefs' blowtorch, or place them under a hot grill/broiler. When they are ready, they should be a deep orange-brown. Allow to cool slightly before serving.

Tartelettes au Citron

These elegant little tartlets are perfect enjoyed with a crisp glass of chilled Champagne for any special celebration.

75 G / ½ CUP SIFTED ICING/CONFECTIONERS' SUGAR, PLUS 4 TABLESPOONS FOR THE TOPPING

175 G / 1 STICK PLUS 4 TABLESPOONS UNSALTED BUTTER, CUBED, AT ROOM TEMPERATURE

½ TEASPOON SALT

2 EGG YOLKS

250 G / 2 CUPS SIFTED PLAIN/ALL-PURPOSE FLOUR

filling and topping:

4 EGGS

150 G / ¾ CUP VANILLA SUGAR

2 TABLESPOONS FINELY GRATED LEMON ZEST

150 G / ⅔ CUP CRÈME FRAÎCHE, PLUS EXTRA TO SERVE

100 ML / ⅓ CUP PLUS 1 TABLESPOON FRESHLY SQUEEZED LEMON JUICE, PLUS 4 TABLESPOONS EXTRA

2 TABLESPOONS MANDARIN OR OTHER CITRUS LIQUEUR

6 loose-bottomed tartlet pans, 9-cm/3½ inches diameter

MAKES 6

To make the pastry, put the icing/confectioners' sugar, butter, salt and egg yolks into the bowl of a food processor. Whizz for 20 seconds.

Add half the flour and pulse to mix; add the remaining flour and pulse again until the texture resembles breadcrumbs. With the machine running, trickle in 2 tablespoons iced water; the dough quickly clumps into a ball. Wrap it in clingfilm/plastic wrap and chill for 20 minutes.

Divide the pastry into 6 equal balls. Dust with flour, then roll them out on a sheet of non-stick baking parchment to a thickness of 5 mm/^{1}/$_4$ inch. Cut each into a circle 10–11 cm/4–4^1/$_2$ inches in diameter.

Preheat the oven to 180°C (350°F) Gas 4.

Place the tartlet pans on a baking sheet. Gently ease the pastry into the pans, letting it sit 1 cm/^{1}/$_2$ inch above the edge: it will shrink slightly as it cooks. Line each pastry case with baking parchment and baking beans or rice. Bake for 15 minutes. Remove the paper and beans, then bake the cases for 5 minutes more.

Now make the filling. Put the eggs, vanilla sugar, half the zest, the crème fraîche, lemon juice and liqueur into a food processor. Pulse in brief bursts until the mixture looks even. Divide it between the 6 pastry cases.

Reduce the oven temperature to 120°C (250°F) Gas ^{1}/$_2$. Bake the tartlets for 15–20 minutes, or until the filling is barely set.

Meanwhile, prepare the topping: put the remaining zest, the 4 tablespoons of icing/confectioners' sugar and the extra lemon juice into a frying pan/skillet. Cook over medium heat until the syrup reduces and is fragrant.

Remove the tartlets from the oven and drizzle this syrup over them. Serve hot, warm or cool, adding a dusting of icing/confectioners' sugar, if liked, and some extra crème fraîche.

Index